The Concise Illustrated Book of
Wild Flowers

Jim Flegg

GALLERY BOOKS
An imprint of W. H. Smith Publishers Inc.
112 Madison Avenue
New York, New York 10016

First published in the United States of America
by GALLERY BOOKS
An imprint of W.H. Smith Publishers Inc.
112 Madison Avenue
New York, New York 10016

ISBN 0-8317-1675-4

Printed in Spain

Acknowledgments

Leo Batten/Frank Lane Picture Agency 41; J.
Allen Cash Ltd. 9; Ron and Christine Foord
20; Harry Fox/Oxford Scientific Films 23;
Peggy Heard/Frank Lane Picture Agency 34;
Eric and David Hosking 14, 44; Tom Leach/
Oxford Scientific Films 24; Ian Rose/Eric and
David Hosking front cover, back cover, 12,
13, 19, 25, 26, 28, 40, 42, 46; Kjell Sandved/
Oxford Scientific Films 22; Harry Smith
Horticultural Photographic Collection 7, 11,
15, 18, 21, 29, 32, 35, 36, 38, 39, 45;
Smith/Polunin Collection 16, 17, 27, 31, 33,
37; Smith/Stainton Collection 10; Roger
Tidman/Frank Lane Picture Agency 4;
Anthony Wharton/Frank Lane Picture Agency
30, 43; David Wrigglesworth/Oxford
Scientific Films 8.

Artwork by Jane Pickering/Linden Artists

CONTENTS

Introduction

Plants play a very significant part in our lives in more ways than one. Plant communities are the essence of the landscape. Just imagine the moonscape nature of our scenery were it to be denuded of plants; the mountains without their cloak of dark green conifers below the pristine whiteness of the snow; a desert island without its coconut palms to cast artistic shadows over coral sands; or a garden without its spring show of flowers.

However, far more important than these aesthetic feelings is the fact that plants are the basis for *all* life on earth. Without the process of photosynthesis which is carried out by all green plants, life would cease. The sun's energy and the simple ingredients of water and carbon dioxide (CO_2) are harnessed by plants, using the catalyst chlorophyll (the active green pigment), to produce the energy for their growth. Amongst other things this complex piece of biochemistry locks up surplus carbon dioxide (forests do this most efficiently; hence our destruction of forests creates the potentially damaging 'greenhouse effect' to our climate caused by excess carbon dioxide). At the same time it releases oxygen and creates a food source, both vital to the animal kingdom. Even the most microscopic of roundworms, parasitic in the blood of its host, ultimately derives its sustenance from the plant matter eaten by that host – either at first or second hand.

Consider just how many plants we humans have taken into cultivation to supply ourselves with food – from the mile-upon-mile of golden corn-clad prairie to the carefully nurtured asparagus bed. We eat roots, shoots, leaves, flowers and fruit from an immense number of plants belonging to a range of botanical families. Other plants have been used as medicines for thousands of years, and it is interesting to see the trend back to using natural plant products and away from materials synthesized in laboratories.

Other plants are admired for their spectacular beauty. An amazing variety of form and colour is to be found among flowers and foliage of different plants. This is often seen at its best where they grow in the wild; for instance the carpets of meadow flowers that dazzle the eye with their kaleidoscopic colours. In detail, too, wild flowers have much to offer, and too few of us too rarely take the trouble to inspect and admire a single wayside bloom at close quarters or use a hand lens to reveal its full glory. On the other hand, there can be few of us who do not admire their cultivated, often more showy relatives. Though the cultivation of cacti and other house plants may be fairly recent, the use of a huge range of plants grown specifically to beautify our living surroundings, whether in our gardens or parks, has been a sign of civilization for centuries.

The world of plants is endlessly fascinating. There are plants for all seasons, plants growing in almost all the world's habitats (even the Antarctic Ice Cap has its own sub-zero-temperature-tolerant alga); plants that parasitize other plants; carnivorous plants that trap and digest insects, and plants that mimic insects in order to be pollinated – like some orchids! How have so many plants become so widespread? Some use their own seed dispersal mechanisms utilizing wind, water or animals, others man has moved as crops or as ornamentals – or, unintentionally and disastrously, as weeds! Examples of some of these varied plants found growing wild fill the pages that follow.

Sagittaria sagittifolia

Classification: Angiospermae – Monocotyledones; Alismataceae
Habitat: Ponds, ditches, canals and slow-moving rivers
Distribution: Irregularly distributed through temperate Europe, Asia and North America
Season: Flowers July and August
Description: An elegant water plant, overwintering by means of egg-shaped turion buds 3cm (1 in) in diameter, bright blue with yellow spots. Submerged leaves strap-like and translucent, floating leaves oval, aerial leaves on long stems, broadly arrow-shaped, up to 20cm (8 in) long.

Flowers carried on tall emergent stems in whorls of three to five, each 2cm (4/5 in) across with three circular white petals and numerous purple stamens. The female flowers smaller than the male, with shorter stalks and form the lower whorls of the inflorescence. Head of carpels knobbly, almost spherical, purplish and about 15mm (³⁄₅ in) diameter. Perennial.

General Remarks: The Pteridophyta (ferns and horsetails) are relatively primitive plants with an alternation of generations; the sporophyte (fern) produces spores on the fronds, which in turn produce a prothallus, much smaller and producing the two sex cells. More advanced are the seed-bearing plants, the Gymnospermae, which include the conifers (not in this text) and the Angiospermae, the flowering plants. The Angiospermae is the most sophisticated class of plants where the ovule is completely enclosed in an ovary. It is divided into two groups, the Dicotyledones with a pair of cotyledons or seedling leaves, and the Monocotyledones with a single cotyledon. The dicot leaf normally has a branching network of veins; in the monocot, the veins are usually parallel.

BLUE IRIS

Iris versicolor

Classification: Angiospermae – Monocotyledones: Iridaceae
Habitat: Swamps, lake, stream and slow-moving river banks
Distribution: North America; initially introduced but now naturalized in parts of north-western Europe
Season: Flowers June and July
Description: Robust grey-green stems rise 50cm (20 in) (to 1m – 39 in – in exceptional circumstances) from a slender rhizome 1cm (⅖ in) in diameter. Succeeding generations of flowers originate from a series of lateral buds on the rhizome. Leaves lance-shaped, sheathing the stem, not differentiated into petiole and blade. Each stem carries up to three showy flowers, up to 8cm (3 in) across, generally pale blue, often tinged pink or purple.

Flowers tri-radiate in structure, with the three outer perianth segments (called 'falls') downcurved and larger than the three upright inner segments (called 'standards') with a limb and claw of equal length. Ovary is three-celled, maturing to a miniature gherkin shape about 4cm (1⅗ in) long, which splits open and reflexes at the end of the summer to reveal large spherical seeds. Perennial.

General Remarks: The Iridaceae, with about 1,000 species grouped in 70 genera, is cosmopolitan in distribution and a family of great horticultural importance. Many of the natural species have been taken into garden or commercial cut-flower cultivation, and others are the parents of a large range of ornamental cultivars. Irises can also be 'forced' by manipulating temperature and day length to give a greatly extended cut-flower season. Also included in this family are crocuses (*Crocus*), montbretia (*Crocosmia*), *Romulea*, *Sisyrhinchium*, and gladioli (*Gladiolus*).

BULL THISTLE (SPEAR THISTLE)

Cirsium vulgare

Classification: Angiospermae – Dicotyledones; Compositae
Habitat: Fields, pastures, roadside and track verges, open waste land
Distribution: Temperate regions of Europe and western Asia to about 70°N; northern Africa. Introduced to temperate zones of both North and South America
Season: Flowers July to October
Description: A substantial tap root and basal rosette of winter leaves produces a stem up to 150cm (60 in) tall, often with several branches. Stems dark green, deeply furrowed, with several wings heavily armed with purplish brown spines. Rosette leaves dark green, up to 30cm (12 in) long, slender and lance-shaped, deeply pinnate with an undulating margin and plentiful spines. Stem leaves similar, sessile, with a downy undersurface.

Flowering heads up to 5cm (2 in) deep, 4cm (1½ in) in diameter. Involucre pale green and bulbous, armed with many dark green spiny hairs. Florets all similar, reddish purple. Biennial.

General Remarks: The Compositae is the largest family of flowering plants in the world, with 14,000 species in 900 genera. It contains annual and perennial herbs, climbers, shrubs and trees, with examples living in most habitats, from deserts to lakes and seashores to mountainsides.

The key feature of this vast assemblage is the compound flower structure; each flower is a composite of many florets – hence the name Compositae. Some (e.g. the thistles) have only tubular florets, while others (e.g. Golden Rod) have a compound central disc of tubular flowers surrounded by an outer ring of ligulate ray florets, so called because of their strap-like 'petal'.

CHICORY

Cichorium intybus

Classification: Angiospermae – Dicotyledones; Compositae

Habitat: Roadsides, rough pastures, open grassland, especially on calcareous soils

Distribution: Probably native to much of Europe north to Scandinavia, central Russia, western Asia; probably introduced to South Africa, Australia, and North and South America

Season: Flowers July to October

Description: Stiff, grooved and bristly branched green stems rise 1m (39 in) or more from a deep tap root. Leaves bright green, bristly, spear-shaped, usually sessile, up to 8cm (3 in) long with smooth margins. Lower leaves often pinnate or deeply toothed. Flowering heads up to 5cm (2 in) across, usually carried in twos or threes on short stems. Florets bright blue, all ligulate, up to 2cm (¾ in) long with a toothed tip. Flowers open early morning, close by noon. Perennial.

General Remarks: Hardly surprisingly because of the size and diversity of the family, the Compositae contains many of the most popular ornamental garden plants, including *Helianthus, Rudbeckia, Dahlia, Chrysanthemum, Tagetes, Gaillardia, Doronicum, Erigeron, Aster* and *Cosmos.*

Many others are widely cultivated as vegetables, including *Cichorium* (chicory and endive), *Lactuca* (lettuce), *Helianthus tuberosus* (Jerusalem artichoke), and the oil-seed-bearing sunflower, *Sigesbeckia.*

Most Compositae are insect pollinated; the seeds are numerous, of a slim cigar-shape, often with a parachute-like feathery pappus to aid wind dispersal (as in the thistles). Other seeds have hooked or barbed bristles or spines to facilitate dispersal by animals, e.g. *Bidens*, (bur marigolds) and *Arctium* (burdocks).

COMFREY

Symphytum officinale

Classification: Angiospermae – Dicotyledones; Boraginaceae
Habitat: Damp open places, water meadows, lakesides and open deciduous woodland
Distribution: Widespread across temperate Europe and Asia; introduced as a herb to North America
Season: Flowers in May and June
Description: A distinctive rough, hairy herb rising in clumps up to 1m (39 in) from a massive fleshy rootstock. Stem grey-green, hairy, winged. Leaves lance-shaped, with a long petiole, up to 25cm (10 in) long, mid-green and bristly. Flowers in characteristic curled clusters of ten or more. Calyx of sharply pointed sepals, about 8mm (⅓ in) long, enclosing a tubular corolla twice that length, with a protruding style. Flower colour variable, commonly white or blue, occasionally yellowish or pinkish.

General Remarks: Enjoying local names such as 'Abraham, Isaac and Joseph' and 'Coffee Flower', Comfrey has a reputation amongst herbalists and country folk since medieval times for its list of actual or reputed medicinal powers. These range from poultices designed to extract the most stubborn of splinters, to healing ruptures and even backaches caused by any form of over-exertion (including, in John Gerard's *Herbal*, published in 1597, 'over-much use of women, doth in fower or five daies perfectly cure the same . . .'). Its most popular use was in setting fractured bones. The massive Comfrey root was ground up and made into a papier-mache-like paste, which quickly set rock hard – an effective precursor of today's plaster cast.

CORAL-ROOT

Corallorhiza trifida

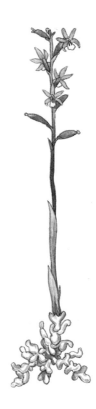

Classification: Angiospermae – Monocotyledones; Orchidaceae
Habitat: Birch, pine and alder woods on peaty soils, and on sand-dunes
Distribution: Much of Europe; Siberia; North America
Season: Flowers May to August
Description: Extraordinary whitish rhizomes with multiple rounded lobes, with the appearance of pieces of coral. Stem yellowish, rising up to 20cm (8 in), with lower half protected by up to four brown sheathing scales with prominent dark brown veins. Leaves absent. Raceme of up to 12 small flowers. Bracts tiny, yellowish green; ovary carried on short twisted stalk, elongated, about 7mm (¼ in) long.

Flowers yellowish or whitish, sometimes with reddish brown margins or spots. Lip strap-like, about 5mm (⅕ in) long, other perianth segments triangular or narrowly triangular; these and the hood are much the same length as the lip. Perennial.

General Remarks: Coral-root is one of a small genus of saprophytic orchids. Saprophytes draw essential nutrients from dying, dead and decaying material in the soil. They lack the vital pigment chlorophyll, present in most plant leaves and stems, giving them their green coloration. Chlorophyll, located within plant cells in chloroplasts, is the vital (and unique) catalyst that allows green plants to convert carbon dioxide and water into carbohydrates using sunlight as an energy source. This is truly vital, because ultimately life on earth is dependent on this process in green plants. Lacking chlorophyll, saprophytes are usually pallid, yellowish or brownish in colour.

CORN COCKLE

Agrostemma githago

Classification: Angiospermae – Dicotyledones; Caryophyllaceae
Habitat: Cereal and other arable fields and field headlands
Distribution: Probably originated in the Mediterranean basin as a plant of open arid land, now widely dispersed as an accidental introduction with cereal seed throughout the temperate regions of the globe. Naturalized in Europe, North America and elsewhere
Season: Flowers June to August
Description: An upright slender mid-green herb, 30–60cm (12–24 in)

tall. Stems often unbranched, hairy, bearing pairs of slender spear-like leaves, sessile and embracing the stem with slightly swollen leaf bases. Each leaf 5–12cm (2–5 in) long, hairy.

Flowers striking, 3–5cm (1–2 in) in diameter, usually solitary. Calyx tube hairy, with ten prominent ribs, with long, slim, spreading, pointed leaf-like teeth often extending up to 5cm (2 in) between petals. Petals purple, heart-shaped. Capsule cylindrical, longer than calyx tube, containing seeds about 3mm (⅛ in) across, black with a warty surface. Visited by butterflies but automatically self-pollinated. Annual.

General Remarks: Rapidly decreasing as a cereal weed due to the use of modern herbicides. As pressures to maximize cereal production decrease, so the Corn Cockle may make a come-back similar to that of the Field Poppy. 'Cockled seeds' are said to be poisonous, but confusion may occur with cereal seeds themselves which turn dark and warty when infested with *Anguina*, a microscopic plant parasite carried in the soil by nemotodes. It is such seeds whose fertility has been destroyed, that Shakespeare refers to when he wrote 'Sow'd cockle, reaped no corn'.

CRANBERRY

Vaccinium oxycoccus (Oxycoccus palustris)

Classification: Angiospermae – Dicotyledones; Ericaceae
Habitat: Peaty bogs, occasionally damp heathland and tundra, normally on acid soils
Distribution: Circumpolar in sub-Arctic, cool-temperate and temperate zones, from Europe through Asia to Japan; North America south to North Carolina, Wisconsin and British Colombia; Greenland
Season: Flowers June to August; fruits ripen August to October
Description: A low-growing or prostrate small woody evergreen shrub, with slender but slightly flexible stems, rooting at intervals along their length. Leaves elongate-oval, up to 1cm (½ in) long, widely spaced in pairs, strongly convex, dark green above, hairy and silvery green below.

Pendant flowers carried on long slender stems, up to 3cm (1¼ in) long, bearing a pair of bracteoles near the middle; four narrow, pointed petals, 6mm (¼ in) long and pink. Fruit fleshy, roughly spherical, up to 1cm (½ in) diameter (up to 2cm – ⅘ in in cultivars), red or reddish brown. Perennial.

General Remarks: Though the Ericaceae may be best-known as the family containing the heathers and heaths, other components of this large assembly (1,500 species in 80 genera) include the spectacular rhododendrons so popular in cultivation and *Arctostaphylos*, which includes the Bearberry, and various *Vaccinium* species. These include species important as berry-bearing food plants in moorland and tundra ecosystems, such as Cowberry, Bilberry, Huckleberry, Whortleberry and Cranberry.

Many of these berries are also favoured for human consumption, none more so than the Cranberry species used to make cranberry jelly.

DAY LILY

Hemerocallis fulva

Classification: Angiospermae – Monocotyledones; Liliaceae
Habitat: Open woodland, woodland fringes and moist scrubby areas
Distribution: Japan and Siberia, perhaps western North America, but widely introduced elsewhere
Season: Flowers July and August
Description: A mass of tuberous rhizomes produce large clumps of leaves and flowering stems, often 1m (39 in) across.

Leaves pale yellowish green, narrowly sword-shaped, with numerous parallel whitish veins; deeply folded in

a V; 60cm (24 in) or longer.

Flowers borne on stout stems, in clusters of six or more opening in turn, each one lasting but a day. Trumpet-shaped and 10cm (4 in) across, they are rich red with an apricot throat. Three elongate-oval petaloid sepals support three broader petals, each reflexed over a central ridge. Six long gold-tipped orange stamens surround an apricot style 7cm (3 in) long. Seed capsule elongate, up to 3cm (1 in) long. Perennial.

General Remarks: The Liliaceae is a cosmopolitan family, with some 2,500 species in 200 genera. Though outwardly their appearances may differ greatly, closer inspection shows the three-petals, three-sepals trumpet-shaped flower to be a constant factor, even if a hand lens is necessary.

As well as the highly ornamental day lilies, the Liliaceae contain the true lilies, tulips, fritillaries, autumn crocuses, grape hyacinths and *Ornithogalums*, all represented in gardens and popular for their flowers and sometimes rich scent. The family also contains the onions (*Allium*) of both ornamental and culinary use, as well as garlic, and asparagus, one of the most delectable of vegetables.

FIELD POPPY

Papaver rhoeas

Classification: Angiospermae – Dicotyledones; family Papaveraceae

Habitat: Occurs naturally as a colonist of freshly-exposed soils (e.g. after fires or landslides). Adapted readily to arable farming, so now widespread as a 'weed' of cereal crops and adjacent headlands

Distribution: Much of temperate Europe and Asia, and North Africa. Introduced into North America, New Zealand and Australia

Season: Flowers from May onwards until autumn, but particularly from June to August

Description: A slender green or grey-green herb with branched stems rising 20–60cm (8–24 in) from a slim tap root. Lower leaves stalked, usually cut pinnately into a number of spear-shaped segments. Upper leaves sessile, spear-shaped with only minor pinnate cuts. Leaves may be smooth or hairy.

Flowers of four roughly circular slightly crinkled petals, up to 10cm (4 in) diameter, usually scarlet, occasionally crimson, pink or white, often with blackish 'eye', supported by two cupped green sepals with bristly exterior surfaces. Bluish anthers borne on slender filaments. Seed capsule strikingly large and lantern-like, twice as long as it is broad, containing many blackish spherical seeds. No nectar but visited frequently by pollen-collecting bees. Self-incompatible. Annual, very variable in hairiness and colour.

General Remarks: In the past, a serious and often abundant weed of cereal fields, often covering them with scarlet blooms. Thirty years of intensified farming using extensive herbicide applications, almost eliminated the Field Poppy. Reduced herbicide usage, however, has now led to its widespread return.

Solidago virgaurea

Classification: Angiospermae – Dicotyledones; Compositae
Habitat: Catholic, including dry grassland, open woodland, sea cliffs, mountain screes, hedges and sand dunes; and on almost any soil type
Distribution: Widespread in temperate Europe, Asia and North America, including montane regions
Season: Flowers June to September
Description: Robust green flowering stems rise up to 75cm (30 in), bearing many long slender spear-shaped leaves with short stout petioles, up to 10cm (4 in) long, with margins that

may be smooth or serrated to various degrees.

Flowers grouped into either a panicle or a raceme. Flowers carried on short stems, arising from the axils of short bracts. The flowers themselves are compound, with a central disc of rayless florets about 4mm (⅙ in) across, surrounded by up to 12 rayed petal-like florets each about 6mm (¼ in) long to give a yellow daisy-like appearance. Perennial.

General Remarks: Though *Solidago virgaurea* is a handsome plant, it is *S. canadensis* that is the basis of the commonly cultivated garden form of Golden Rod. A native of North America, it is now widely naturalized following its 'escape' from introductions into Europe.

S. virgaurea itself is an extremely variable species, with plants from severe montane habitats growing to little more than 5cm (2 in). The degree of hairiness; the size, shape and marginal serration of the leaves; and the size and structure of the flowering head are all also variable and have given rise to several named races or varieties.

GREAT REEDMACE (BULRUSH)

Typha latifolia

Classification: Angiospermae – Monocotyledones; Typhaceae

Habitat: Often dominant in muddy ponds and lakes, reed swamps, ditches, slow-moving rivers, and canals

Distribution: Circumglobal, from the Arctic Circle to the Tropic of Capricorn at 30°S, but absent from central and southern Africa and Australasia

Season: Flowers appear in June and July, shedding seeds in February and March

Description: Stout rhizomes up to 8cm (3 in) diameter, well rooted, spread rapidly through muddy shallows. From these, straight simple stems rise to often over 2m (6½ ft), with many broad – up to 5cm (2 in) – long sword-shaped leaves.

Inflorescence in two adjacent parts, both compound, male uppermost. Male component is catkin-like, 10cm (4 in) or more long, often droopng. Female component is cylindrical, up to 3cm (1¼ in) diameter by 20cm (8 in) long, smooth and velvety, initially green, turning dark brown. Perennial.

General Remarks: A well-known and spectacular water plant, this is often a problem in wetland conservation areas because of its ability to spread rapidly and crowd out other more sensitive plants. Eventually this may lead to the drying-out of ponds and colonization by woody plants like alders (*Alnus*) or sallows (*Salix*). This is not, however, the bulrush of the Biblical account of the finding of the baby Moses: that would have been in a papyrus swamp. The Typhaceae is a small family (nine species in a single genus) and is distinct from both the sedges (Cyperaceae) and the reeds (e.g. *Phragmites*) which fall within the grass family, Gramineae.

GREATER BLADDERWORT

Utricularia vulgaris

Classification: Angiospermae – Dicotyledones; Lentibulariaceae
Habitat: Freshwater lakes, ponds and deeper ditches, often in montane areas
Distribution: Temperate regions of Europe, northern Africa, Asia and North America
Season: Flowers July and August
Description: Slender floating stems up to 50cm (20 in) long carry finely pinnately divided green leaves up to 25mm (1 in) long, each with several trap-bladders about 3mm (⅛ in) in

diameter. Flowering stalks up to 20cm (8 in) tall, bearing up to eight flowers, rise above the surface from the leaf axils.

Flowers bright gold, 15mm (⅗ in) or more in diameter, with a complexly bulbous lower lip and a smaller, roughly oval upper lip. The plant is perennial.

General Remarks: The Lentibulariaceae is a small family (250 species in five genera) of varied insect-eating plants, mostly in two genera, *Pinguicula* (butterworts), which have sticky leaves, and about 200 species in *Utricularia* (bladderworts), of which most occur in the tropics. Superficially the flowers of the Lentibulariaceae resemble those of the Scrophulariaceae, but the families are separated by the insectivorous habits of the former, and by anatomical differences within the ovary.

The Greater Bladderwort is a free-floating plant, lacking roots, but obtaining essential nutrients (other than those obtained by photosynthesis) from small water animals such as water fleas (*Daphnia*) which it traps in its underwater bladders. It overwinters as turions, special detachable well-protected buds that fall to the lake bottom.

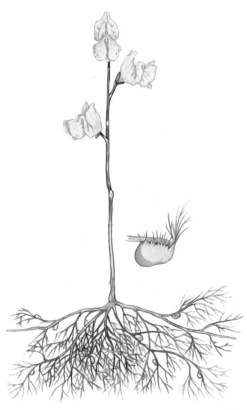

HEDGEHOG CACTUS

Echinocereus spp.

Classification: Angiospermae – Dicotyledones; Cactaceae

Habitat: Deserts and other lowland arid areas subject to infrequent but heavy rains

Distribution: Southern North America, Central America; in cultivation worldwide

Season: Flowers irregularly dependent on conditions

Description: A deeply penetrating root system supports clusters of cylindrical stems up to 25cm (10 in) long and 5cm (2 in) in diameter. The succulent stem is leafless, slightly furrowed, grey-green and smoothly fleshy, protected by numerous areoles bearing clusters of four to six sharp, rigid whitish spines 1cm (⅖ in) or more long, arranged along the ridges.

Flowers are comparatively large, up to 8cm (3 in) across, stemless and conical, usually pink or yellow, made up of a great number of petals and a similar number of prominent stamens; the stigma is also prominent. Perennial.

General Remarks: The Cactaceae are native to southern North America, Central America, and northern South America, but have naturalized well in warm temperate and tropical climates worldwide, not always as arid as their native deserts. Succulent stems store water taken up during occasional torrential rains. They are green because they contain chlorophyll to carry out the necessary photosynthesis to provide life-support for the cactus, rendering leaves (with their potential for losing precious water) superfluous. Spines are essential to protect such a rich and accessible water source from thirsty animals. *Echinocereus* species have various spectacular flower colours and are popular house plants.

Equisetum arvense

Classification: Pteridophyta; Equisitaceae

Habitat: Fields, rough grassland, banks, damp soils, dune slacks; up to 900m (3,000 ft)

Distribution: Widespread in the northern Hemisphere in a circumpolar belt stretching south from the Arctic to Spain and Greece in Europe; to Virginia, Alabama and California in North America

Season: Spores shed in April

Description: Rhizome hairy, with oval tubers. Sterile stems rise to 1m (39 in), 5mm (⅕ in) or more across, green, rough and deeply grooved. Branches numerous, green, arranged in flat rosettes, 5–10cm (2–4 in) long. Leaves small, about 5mm (⅕ in) long, grouped in sheaths at nodes, green with blackish tips, giving stems and branches a segmented appearance. Fertile stems simple and unbranched, pallid brown, 10–25cm (4–10 in), topped with a 4cm (2 in) spore-containing cone-like structure. Perennial.

General Remarks: With 23 species in a single genus, the horsetails are remarkably cosmopolitan, absent only from Australasia and Antarctica. They are ancient plants and plentiful fossil evidence links the horsetails of today with the humid swamps in which gigantic dinosaurs flourished hundreds of millions of years ago.

In medieval times, horsetails were renowned as effective dressings for battle wounds; provided a source of green and yellow dyes; and were used as kitchen pot scourers which utilized their natural abrasiveness. This roughness is due to myriad fine silica crystals on the plant surface, which has led to them being used down the ages for finishing and polishing such diverse materials as armour and fine marquetry.

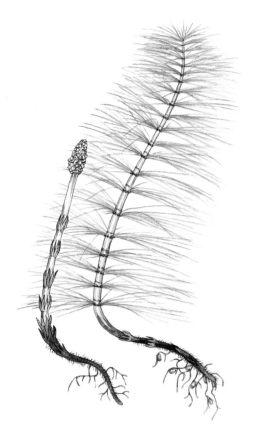

INDIAN PIPE (PITCHER PLANT)

Sarracenia purpurea

Classification: Angiospermae – Dicotyledones; Sarraceniaceae
Habitat: Peaty swamps and bogs
Distribution: Native to eastern North America; introduced, now naturalized and often abundant first in Ireland, then elsewhere in Europe as far east as Switzerland
Season: Flowers April to June
Description: A stout low-growing evergreen plant forming tussocks about 25cm (10 in) high and 30cm (12 in) across. Leaves conspicuous, stemless, up to 15 cm (6 in) long and formed into jug- or pitcher-like shapes, bulbously tubular, narrowing near the top then expanding with a spreading lip, pale green with prominent reddish purple veins. Flowering stems slender, 15–40cm (6–16 in) tall, carrying a single flower or a few in a raceme.

Flowers drooping, cup-shaped, up to 5cm (2 in) across. Strap-like sepals, longer than rounded petals, all being purplish green. Style comparatively huge, umbrella-shaped, about 3cm (1¼ in) in diameter. Perennial.

General Remarks: In common with some other plants of peaty soils lacking vital nutrients, the Sarraceniaceae have turned to carnivorous habits to supplement their diet. Insects lured by tempting secretions are trapped by the slippery-sided pitchers, fall into the basal fluid and are digested, to be absorbed by the leaf. Most families with pitcher-like leaf structures and carnivorous habits are tropical, commonly African or Asian. Many, including several *Sarracenia* species, are popular house or cool greenhouse plants.

Sarracenia purpurea is probably the most northerly pitcher plant, and thus in frost-free areas naturalized populations have been successfully established and now flourish.

Arum maculatum

Classification: Angiospermae – Monocotyledones; Araceae
Habitat: Woodland, dense hedge-rows. Usually in shaded and often in damp locations, favouring alkaline soils
Distribution: Northern and western Europe, northern Africa. Introduced in North America
Season: Flowers April and May, fruits conspicuous July and August
Description: Dark green, fleshy and shiny leaves rise from a tuber about 25mm (1 in) long. Leaves arrow-shaped, up to 20cm (8 in) long, often

black or brown-spotted. Flowering spike (spadix) sheathed in a leaf-like spathe, up to 25cm (10 in) tall, erect and conspicuously pale yellowish green, often edged or spotted with purple, occasionally almost white. Base of spathe bulbous, enclosing the tiny female flowers. Spadix up to 12cm (5 in) long, pencil-like and about 8mm (1/3 in) across. The visible section is dull purple, rarely yellow, and carries many tiny male flowers.

The fruits, strikingly orange, spherical and about 5mm (1/5 in) dia-meter, ripen within the bulbous region and the spathe withers, bursting out in late summer as a spike carrying up to 20 fruits. Perennial.

General Remarks: Jack-in-the-pulpit arises either from the striking spring appearance of the purple spadix within the pale spathe, or from the stem of bright orange and highly poisonous berries, upright and prom-inent against the drying spathe in late summer. Cross-pollination is the rule in *Arum*, with insects lured by nectar into the spathe. There they slither down and are trapped in the bulbous section until pollination, properly timed, is complete. Some members of the Araceae are cultivated as house plants for their spectacular foliage.

LADY'S SLIPPER ORCHID

Cypripedium calceolus

Classification: Angiospermae – Monocotyledones; Orchidaceae
Habitat: Old-established broad-leaved woodlands on limestone or other basic rocks
Distribution: Temperate regions of the Northern Hemisphere; now rare in many places because of its attraction to plant collectors
Season: Flowers May and June
Description: The rich green, slightly hairy, leafy stems may rise up to 40cm (16 in) (but usually less) from a network of creeping rhizomes. Three or four leaves, pointedly oval, up to 15cm (6 in) long, furrowed above and ridged below along parallel veins, sheathe the flowering stems.

One or rarely two flowers of very distinctive form, 5cm (2 in) or more across. Five or more elongated, spear-shaped purple sepals, the uppermost is broader than the others; the lateral pair twisted; the lower pair fused along much of their length. Lip (labellum) yellow, with darker veins, broad and slipper- or boat-shaped, with anthers drooping into the cavity. Pollen granular, not held in tetrads in pollinia as in most orchids. Perennial.
General Remarks: Best-known for their exotic tropical blooms, and their numerous, glamorous commercial hybrids, the Orchidaceae present an image of exclusivity which is belied by the sheer variety of the family, which with 800 genera and 20,000 species, is second in size only to the Compositae. Many are not as conspicuous and elegant as the Lady's Slipper. Some (*Ophrys*) have flowers that mimic insects so well that they are pollinated during attempted insect matings with the inflated lower lip. Orchid seeds are exceptionally numerous and minute, often requiring special fungal associates (mycorrhiza) for germination and growth.

Cardamine pratensis

Classification: Angiospermae – Dicotyledones; Cruciferae
Habitat: Damp meadows, ditches, freshwater marsh and woodland fringes
Distribution: Widespread through temperate Europe, Asia and North America
Season: An early-season plant flowering from March to June
Description: Overwinters as a compressed rosette of leaves based on a short, well-rooted stock with occasional stolons. Basal leaves are stalked, smooth or slightly hairy,

pinnate, with roughly circular leaflets. Stem leaves also pinnate, with very short stalks and smaller, lance-like leaflets.

Flowers are carried in a corymb of up to 20 florets on smooth stems rising from 15cm (6 in) to 60cm (24 in) in favourable conditions. Each flower is 12–18mm across (½–¾ in) with four short green sepals edged violet and four petals arranged in a cross, usually pale pink or violet, rarely white, with greenish veins and yellow anthers. As the plant ages, the corymb lengthens to a vertical spike, with needle-like seed pods carried upright on short stalks. Perennial.

General Remarks: The link in the English name Cuckoo Flower to the spring arrival of the well-known summer migrant bird reflects the early flowering season. Another vernacular name, Lady's Smock refers to the petal's similarity to the balloon-like skirts of years gone by. Seed dispersal is wide, the elongate seed pods opening suddenly, coiling spirally from the base and catapulting from the plant.

The Cruciferae are another large, cosmopolitan family of the Northern Hemisphere, with about 2,000 species of mostly ephemeral annuals, in over 200 genera.

MARJORAM

Origanum vulgare

Classification: Angiospermae – Dicotyledones; Labiatae
Habitat: Dry grassland, hedge bases, open scrubland, usually on calcareous soils
Distribution: Much of Europe and the western part of Asia. Introduced to North America
Season: Flowers July to September
Description: An erect herb, with many flowering stems rising 20–70cm (8–28 in) from a densely matted mass of fibrous roots. Oval or pointedly oval mid-green leaves, only slightly hairy, are carried on short petioles in opposite pairs. Lower leaves may be 5cm (2 in) long, the upper ones are usually smaller. Short flowering (and some non-flowering) stems rise from the leaf axils.

The flowering head is a loose pannicle composed of dense cymes of flowers. Bracts are leaf-like but smaller and sessile, bracteoles conspicuously purple. Flower is· a five-lipped pink or pale purple tube, the two upper lips almost fused, with four pink stamens. Flowers up to 8mm (⅓ in) diameter. Perennial.
General Remarks: Though the Labiatae is a large family, with over 3,000 species grouped in 170 genera, it is a clearly defined natural grouping of readily recognizable plants. Key Labiate features include fruits characteristically composed of four nutlets (also in the Boraginaceae, but these have alternate leaves and very different flowers).

The stems of the labiates are quadrangular and often square in cross section. This is also a feature of some Scrophulariaceae, and though some of these may have rather similar flowers, they can always be distinguished by their very different ovaries.

MARRAM GRASS

Ammophila arenaria

Classification: Angiospermae – Monoctyledones; Gramineae
Habitat: Coastal sand dunes
Distribution: Coasts of Europe, northern Africa, North America
Season: Flowers July and August
Description: Stout stems creep extensively through loose sand, rooting at the nodes. Flowering spikes rise up to 1m (39 in) from sheaths of long inrolled, sharp-edged grey-green leaves with very sharp points. The outer side of the rigid, desiccation-resistant leaves is smooth, almost polished, while the inner surface is deeply grooved, with pale grey channels covered in fine hairs between prominent, deeper green parallel veins.

Flowers carried in a panicle, each spikelet about 13mm (½ in) long, densely packed and fox-tail-like, up to 15cm (6 in) long by 2cm (⅘ in) wide. Perennial.

General Remarks: The Gramineae is an enormous family with something like 10,000 species grouped into 600 genera. Although not the largest in terms of species, it may well be the most widespread family, found in practically all environments, and grasses are probably the most numerous flowering plants on earth. Flowers are usually green, and composed of bracts known as glumes, lemmas (with or without an awn) and palea which enclose the flower parts, plus various minor components. They differ appreciably from a 'normal' flower composed of a calyx and corolla (often of sepals and petals respectively).

Ammophila contains only three very similar species, all sand dune specialists and frequently planted to stabilize moving dune systems.

MARSH CINQUEFOIL

Potentilla palustris

Classification: Angiospermae – Dicotyledones; Rosaceae

Habitat: Bogs, moors, wet heathland, fens and freshwater marshes, including montane areas in the south of its range

Distribution: From Iceland and subarctic Russia in northern Europe south to the Pyrennees, Dolomites and Caucasus; through Asia from Armenia to Japan; in North America from the subarctic south to northern California in the west and New Jersey on the eastern seaboard

Season: Flowers May to July

Description: From the overwintering woody creeping rhizome, slender reddish green stems rise to 45cm (18 in). Leaves palmate, lower ones with five or seven leaflets up to 6cm (2 in) long, each with deeply serrated margins, dark reddish green above, greyish and hairy underneath. Upper leaflets usually three in number and smaller. Conspicuous pairs of spearshaped bracts at each leaf base.

Flowers carried on short stalks rising from leaf axils; five pointed sepals about 1.5cm (½ in) long, purple with a green margin, protrude between the five shorter, deep purple oval petals. Perennial.

General Remarks: The Rosaceae is another large family, with about 2,000 species in some 100 genera, cosmopolitan in distribution throughout the temperate regions of the globe. There are some 300 species of *Potentilla* mostly in the Northern Hemisphere. Several are cultivated as garden plants, or used as parents in hybridization programmes to produce both popular garden shrubs and to transfer valuable characteristics to, for example, strawberry cultivars. Most have yellow or white flowers; the rusty red blooms of the Marsh Cinquefoil is an exception.

Caltha palustris

Classification: Angiospermae – Dicotyledones; Ranunculaceae

Habitat: Wet woodlands, freshwater marshes and ditches, growing best in partial shade

Distribution: Widespread over much of temperate and cool-temperate Europe, Eurasia and North America, penetrating north into near-Arctic conditions and up to subalpine altitudes.

Season: Flowers March in south to June or July in sub-Arctic latitudes

Description: A fleshy, dark green plant up to 60cm (24 in) tall, with clusters of rich golden yellow flowers each up to 5cm (2 in) in diameter. Groups of stout stems rise from thick rhizomes. Lower leaves are stalked, triangular to heart-shaped, upper leaves kidney-shaped, often sessile; all with crenate or toothed margins. Perianth of five to eight segments, each golden yellow and up to 25mm (1 in) long. Up to 100 golden stamens. Large seeds 2.5mm (1/10 in) in diameter held in knob-like clusters. This plant spreads by both seed dispersal and by creeping rhizomes. Perennial.

General Remarks: Considered to be one of the most primitive of flowering plants, and extremely variable in plant size, in the size of the flowers, and in the shapes of the leaves and seeds. A popular plant with a great many insects seeking its pollen and nectar, secreted by pairs of shallow depressions on either side of each carpel. The Ranunculaceae is a huge family of over 1,300 species in about 50 genera, cosmopolitan in the Northern Hemisphere, with many Arctic species.

MARSH VIOLET (BOG VIOLET)

Viola palustris

Classification: Angiospermae – Dicotyledones; Violaceae

Habitat: Freshwater bogs, fens, marshes, ditches and pools, wet heathland; up to altitudes exceeding 1,220m (4,000 ft). Favours peaty soils

Distribution: Much of western Europe from Portugal to Scandinavia, mountain areas of North Africa; Iceland and Greenland; North America south to the mountains of New England in the east and Washington State in the west

Season: Flowers April to July

Description: A low growing herb with pale, slender creeping rhizome. Leaves and flowers arise from nodes on the rhizome. Leaves dark green, heart- or kidney-shaped, with slightly serrated margins, up to 5cm (2 in) long carried on petioles also up to 5cm (2 in) in length.

Flowers up to 15mm ($\frac{3}{5}$ in) across, of typical 'violet' form, with a prominent lower lip flanked on either side by a pair of smaller petals, pale purple or lilac with darker veins especially prominent on lip. Spur comparatively short but rich in nectar attracting pollinating bees and other insects. Sepals small, roughly oval, green. Seed capsule lacking hairs but with three ridges. When ripe this falls to the ground liberating numerous seeds.

General Remarks: The Violaceae form a well-defined family with no evidently closely-related groups. In all there are about 800 species in less than 20 genera, including herbs, shrubs and some trees. The largest genus is *Viola*, containing half of the named species, all of them relatively small herbs. Most *Viola* produce cleistogamous flowers after the normal flowering season. These lack petals, do not open and are self-fertile.

Stachys palustris

Classification: Angiospermae – Dicotyledones; Labiatae
Habitat: Beside damp ditches, slow-running streams and in freshwater swampy areas, occasionally in recently drained areas.
Distribution: Throughout Europe from Norway in the north to Spain, Italy and Greece; temperate Asia eastward to Japan; temperate North America
Season: Flowers from June or July, until September in the north
Description: Flowering stems rise up

to 1m (39 in) from an extensive network of creeping, copiously-rooted rhizomes. Leaves grey-green arranged in opposing pairs on a square hairy stem, narrowly spear-shaped, sessile and with serrated margins, up to 13cm (5 in) long. Bracts leaf-like but smaller, in pairs supporting a ring of about six flowers, with many such rings to each spike up to 30cm (12 in) long. Calyx grey-green, hairy, about 8mm (⅓ in) long, with five spike-like teeth. Corolla tubular, about 15mm long, pale lilac or dull purple, two upper lips fused into typical hood; central lip expanded and convex, with intricate patterns of white markings; two lateral lips much smaller. Perennial.

General Remarks: Two origins have been suggested for the name Woundwort. One draws attention to the pattern of markings on the corolla lip (particularly prominent in *Stachys sylvatica* and likens them to the nail-mark wounds inflicted on Christ during the Crucifixion.

The other considers that the absorbent and medicinal herbal properties of the genus led to it being used in medieval times as a wound dressing for the bloody injuries caused by sword or spear suffered in battles.

MOSS CAMPION

Silene acaulis

Classification: Angiospermae – Dicotyledones; Caryophyllaceae

Habitat: An arctic-alpine plant of screes, rocky crevices and ledges in mountainous areas; rocky places at lower-altitudes including sea cliffs and gravel drifts in sub-arctic and arctic zones, penetrating at least to 86°N in Greenland.

Distribution: Circumpolar; northern temperate and arctic regions of Europe, Asia and North America

Season: Flowers in July and August

Description: A prostrate, creeping, much branched herb forming dark green moss-like cushions from 2–10cm (1–4 in) high. Leaves form dense rosettes, each leaf about 1cm (⅖ in) long, slender and pointed at the tip, bristly towards the base.

Flowers solitary, about 12mm (½ in) in diameter carried on short stalks just above the leaf cushion. Calyx bulbous, typical of the campion family, often reddish, paper-like. Five petals, deep rose-pink, occasionally paler, each a slender pear-shape, the tip clearly indented to form two lobes. Seed capsule about twice the length of the calyx, opening to shed seeds through six upright teeth. Perennial.

General Remarks: *Silene* is one of the 70 genera of the Caryophyllaceae, a family falling into two subfamilies, the Alsinoideae and the Caryphylloideae. The former contains unscented flat flowers – the chickweeds, for example – with nectar readily accessible to short-tongued insects. The Caryophylloideae contains the campions and the pinks and only the longest-tongued moths can reach the nectar at the base of the deep tubular flowers. The powerful scent of this group is produced largely at night, thus attracting the night-flying moths which are ideal pollinators.

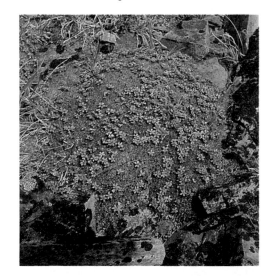

ORANGE BALSAM

Impatiens capensis

Classification: Angiospermae – Dicotyledones; Balsaminaceae

Habitat: Stream and river banks, lakesides

Distribution: Native of the eastern states of North America; from Newfoundland and Saskatchewan in Canada, south to Florida and Nebraska in the United States. Introduced to western Europe; now widespread in Great Britain and still spreading

Season: Flowers June to August

Description: A herb with erect, fleshy, almost translucent pinkish green stems, swollen at the nodes, rising to 50cm (20 in) but often shorter. Leaves mid-green, stalked, roughly egg-shaped, with coarsely serrated margins, 3–8cm (1–3 in) long.

The pendant flowers are produced in ones or twos on slender, arching stems rising from the leaf axils. The flowers are a striking orange with brown blotching in the throat, conical in shape, narrowing to slender spur with an abrupt upward or downward curve, about 3cm (1 in) long overall. Seed pods 2cm (⅘ in) or longer, cucumber-like with prominent longitudinal ridges. Seeds are dispersed as pod splits open from tip and coils elastically, particularly if touched when ripe, catapulting seeds some distance. Annual.

General Remarks: The Balsaminaceae is a comparatively small family with just two genera; *Impatiens* has about 200 species, the other just a single species. The majority come from tropical Africa and Asia, with a few in northern temperate latitudes.

The distinctive shape of the flowers reflects the isolation of the Balsaminaceae from other families. The explosive nature of ripe dehiscing seed capsules has given some the popular name of touch-me-not.

Classification: Angiospermae – Dicotyledones; Scrophulariaceae
Habitat: Open land, dry sunny banks, roadsides and waste places
Distribution: Much of Europe and Asia east to China. Possibly native, more probably introduced and now naturalized in North America
Season: Flowers June to August
Description: An impressively tall plant, sometimes reaching 2m (6½ ft), its flowering stem rising from a rosette of oval to lance-shaped leaves up to 40cm (16 in) long. Stem leaves smaller and narrower, closely packed.

Leaves and stem densely covered with soft whitish woolly hairs, giving the whole plant a striking and characteristic greyish appearance at a distance.

Flowers rich yellow 1.5–3cm (⅗–1⅖ in) diameter, of five roughly equal-sized rounded petals supported by five green triangular sepals. The five stamens, the reddish filaments of the lowest two being longer than the upper three, are covered in white hairs. Flowers borne in a densely packed spike-like raceme, often with secondary branches, up to 1m (39 in) or more in length. Biennial.

General Remarks: Though the Scrophulariaceae is a large (2,500 species in some 200 genera) and anatomically diverse family, most of its members are generally recognizable by their tubular flowers, with a protruding, often bulbous lower lip to the corolla. Popular garden members in use are calceolarias, xiemesias, penstemons, and antirrhinums, widely grown worldwide; while typical wild members include the toadflaxes, figworts and monkey-flowers. *Verbascum* is atypical in possessing a more or less flat corolla.

Verbascum thapsus

Classification: Angiospermae – Dicotyledones; Scrophulariaceae
Habitat: Open land, dry sunny banks, roadsides and waste places
Distribution: Much of Europe and Asia east to China. Possibly native, more probably introduced and now naturalized in North America
Season: Flowers June to August
Description: An impressively tall plant, sometimes reaching 2m (6½ ft), its flowering stem rising from a rosette of oval to lance-shaped leaves up to 40cm (16 in) long. Stem leaves smaller and narrower, closely packed.

Leaves and stem densely covered with soft whitish woolly hairs, giving the whole plant a striking and characteristic greyish appearance at a distance.

Flowers rich yellow 1.5–3cm (³⁄₅–1²⁄₅ in) diameter, of five roughly equal-sized rounded petals supported by five green triangular sepals. The five stamens, the reddish filaments of the lowest two being longer than the upper three, are covered in white hairs. Flowers borne in a densely packed spike-like raceme, often with secondary branches, up to 1m (39 in) or more in length. Biennial.

General Remarks: Though the Scrophulariaceae is a large (2,500 species in some 200 genera) and anatomically diverse family, most of its members are generally recognizable by their tubular flowers, with a protruding, often bulbous lower lip to the corolla. Popular garden members in use are calceolarias, xiemesias, penstemons, and antirrhinums, widely grown worldwide; while typical wild members include the toadflaxes, figworts and monkey-flowers. *Verbascum* is atypical in possessing a more or less flat corolla.

ORANGE BALSAM

Impatiens capensis

Classification: Angiospermae – Dicotyledones; Balsaminaceae
Habitat: Stream and river banks, lakesides
Distribution: Native of the eastern states of North America; from Newfoundland and Saskatchewan in Canada, south to Florida and Nebraska in the United States. Introduced to western Europe; now widespread in Great Britain and still spreading
Season: Flowers June to August
Description: A herb with erect, fleshy, almost translucent pinkish green stems, swollen at the nodes, rising to 50cm (20 in) but often shorter. Leaves mid-green, stalked, roughly egg-shaped, with coarsely serrated margins, 3–8cm (1–3 in) long.

The pendant flowers are produced in ones or twos on slender, arching stems rising from the leaf axils. The flowers are a striking orange with brown blotching in the throat, conical in shape, narrowing to slender spur with an abrupt upward or downward curve, about 3cm (1 in) long overall. Seed pods 2cm (⅘ in) or longer, cucumber-like with prominent longitudinal ridges. Seeds are dispersed as pod splits open from tip and coils elastically, particularly if touched when ripe, catapulting seeds some distance. Annual.

General Remarks: The Balsaminaceae is a comparatively small family with just two genera; *Impatiens* has about 200 species, the other just a single species. The majority come from tropical Africa and Asia, with a few in northern temperate latitudes.

The distinctive shape of the flowers reflects the isolation of the Balsaminaceae from other families. The explosive nature of ripe dehiscing seed capsules has given some the popular name of touch-me-not.

Lythrum salicaria

Classification: Angiospermae – Dicotyledones; Lythraceae
Habitat: Swampy margins of fresh-water lakes, ditches, slow-moving rivers and streams, fens, marshes and reedbeds
Distribution: Widespread throughout Europe, much of temperate Asia, North Africa and North America
Season: Flowers June to August
Description: A straight stem, often without branches, rises up to 1m (39 in) from a bulky fibrous root system. The leaves are spear-shaped and sessile, their bases overlapping the stem,

dark green but moderately hairy, sometimes arranged in threes, sometimes in opposite pairs.

The flowering spike may be 30cm (12 in) or more in length, crowded with whorls of flowers 15–20mm ($\frac{3}{5}$–$\frac{4}{5}$ in) across, the whorls in the axils of small leaf-like bracts. Each flower has five or six slender, crumpled, strap-like purple petals, emerging from a tubular calyx about 6mm (¼ in) long. Perennial.

General Remarks: One of the more spectacular waterside plants, the Purple Loosestrife belongs to a family which although not excessively large (over 500 species in 20 or more genera) contains a range of plants from small annuals through to trees, with representatives throughout the World except in the Arctic and Antarctic regions.

The Purple Loosestrife is found with three distinct flower forms, each occurring on separate plants. One has a short style and long and medium stamens, another has a medium-length style and long and short stamens, the third a long style and short and medium stamens. Each type has a different size of pollen grain.

PURPLE SAXIFRAGE

Saxifraga oppositifolia

Classification: Angiospermae – Dicotyledones; Saxifragaceae
Habitat: Damp rock crevices in montane areas, Arctic tundra gravels. Usually associated with base-rich rocks
Distribution: Circumpolar on Arctic tundra; in alpine areas, up to many thousands of feet in the Alps, the Sierra Nevada and the Apennines, through Central Asia to the Himalayan foothills in Kashmir; the Rocky Mountains in North America south to Vermont
Season: Flowers March to May, occasionally with a second flush in July
Description: Numerous long, prostrate stems and branches forming a compact tussock. Leaves dark green, oval, up to 6mm (¼ in) long, sessile, densely arranged in four rows, each with a lime secreting organ.

Flowers single, terminal, carried on upright stems up to 25mm (1 in) long, about 20mm (⅘ in) in diameter. Five petals, oval, rich pinkish purple; sepals short, green and pointedly oval. Seeds brownish, onion-shaped, up to 6mm (¼ in). Though visited by moths, in many locations probably self-fertile. Perennial.
General Remarks: The Saxifra-gaceae is a cosmopolitan family of about 500 species in 35 genera. Unexpectedly, it includes garden plants like *Bergenia*, *Heuchera* and *Astilbe*, but it is the true saxifrages that are particularly favoured by alpine plant specialists.

Saxifraga is literally translated as 'rock breaker' and reflects the minute cracks in mountain and tundra rocks in which Saxifrages seem readily able to find a satisfactory roothold. The Purple Saxifrage is a particularly spectacular tundra plant, one of the earliest to bloom after the long Arctic winter, producing masses of purple flowers.

Anthriscus sylvestris

Classification: Angiospermae – Dicotyledones; Umbelliferae
Habitat: Particularly beside hedgerows, but also waste land and woodland margins
Distribution: Widespread throughout temperate Europe, in montane areas of southern Europe, east through the Caucasus to Siberia; northern Africa; introduced in North America
Season: Flowers April to June
Description: An upright, much branched herb reaching 1m (39 in), with large, dark green, fern-like pinnate leaves with downy undersides. These are triangular in outline, up to 30cm (12 in) long, with a central stem often hairy beneath, and up to 20 segments arranged in opposite pairs. Each segment is itself pinnatifid, its segments arranged in pairs, up to 25mm (1 in) long, with coarsely serrated margins.

Petiole base winged at its junction with the main stem. Umbels of flowers about 5cm (2 in) diameter, with up to ten rays, 2–5cm (1–2 in) long, arising from a ring of short spear-like bracteoles. Fruit zeppelin-shaped, about 5mm (⅕ in) long, with a short terminal beak. Biennial.

General Remarks: The Umbelliferae is a large family with 3,000 species in 200 genera and cosmopolitan in the Northern Hemisphere. It is also highly distinctive, with the flowers carried in compound umbels on stems resembling the spokes of a miniature umbrella. Most have much-divided fern-like pinnate leaves.

Many have culinary uses; for example the leaves of parsley are used to flavour many dishes, the tap roots of carrot and parsnip are eaten as vegetables. Some are poisonous, like Hemlock, a draught of which was used for the execution of Socrates.

ROYAL FERN

Osmunda regalis

Classification: Pteridophyta; family Osmundaceae

Habitat: Swampy area, wet heaths, damp woodland, usually on peaty soils. Occasionally in drier areas. Up to 365m (1,200 ft)

Distribution: Temperate areas throughout Europe, Asia Minor and Asia; southern Africa; eastern North America from Saskatchewan and Newfoundland southwards

Season: Spores ripen June–August

Description: Rhizome upright and massive, lacking scales. Leaves may rise from 50cm to 3m (20 to 120 in) on petioles that are initially hairy but soon become smooth. Leaves pale green, smooth, roughly lanceolate in outline but bi-pinnate, with up to 15 pairs of pinnae. The lower few pairs of pinnae are usually sterile, the remainder fertile, decreasing in size towards the tip.

Sterile pinnae have pairs of pinnules up to 6cm (2½ in) long; fertile pinnae have pairs of pinnules up to 3cm (1¼ in) long; with irregularly crenate margins and prominent dichotomously branching veins on both surfaces, covered profusely with brown sporangia. Each sporangium contains up to 500 spores, which are shed through a slit, each giving rise to a heart-shaped green prothallus. Perennial.

General Remarks: This is one of the most spectacular of ferns. Though widespread to the point of being almost cosmopolitan, it relatively rarely occurs in dense stands. The Osmundaceae are divided into three genera containing about 20 species in total. It is a favoured plant for cultivation, to the extent that collectors have threatened populations in some areas, leading almost to its extinction.

Hypericum canadense

Classification: Angiospermae – Dicotyledones; Hypericaceae
Habitat: Damp woodlands; peaty swamps; stream, pond and lakesides
Distribution: Temperate areas of western Europe and North America
Season: Flowers July and August
Description: A slender erect herb, growing to 12–25cm (5–10 in). Stems smooth and slender, rich green tinged purple, square in cross-section. Leaves mid-green, delicate, set in opposite pairs clasping the stem, elliptical, with three major veins, up to 1cm (⅖ in) long. Leaf surface copiously spotted with translucent glands.

The flowering head is a raceme, with three to twelve flowers each about 8mm (⅓ in) across. Sepals greenish, with red streaks but lacking black spot-like glands, pointedly spear-shaped, about 4mm (⅙ in) long. Petals about the same length, narrowly oval, rich yellow with a crimson line on the reverse; widely spaced around the dense cluster of reddish gold stamens, giving a characteristically star-like appearance. Annual.

General Remarks: The Hypericaceae is a small but well-defined family of herbaceous plants and shrubs, with over 250 species grouped in eight genera. Most are native of lowland temperate regions or tropical highlands. A number of species, and their hybrids, especially from *Hypericum*, are popular garden plants. *H. calycinum*, the Rose of Sharon or Aaron's Beard, is valuable both for its showy 8cm (3 in) flowers and as weed-excluding ground cover.

Though much smaller-flowered, other *Hypericum* species including *H. canadense* are renowned as wild flowers for their detailed beauty, and well repay close examination.

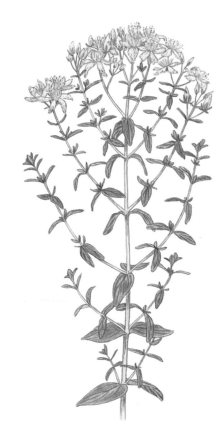

39

SEA BINDWEED

Calystegia (Convolvulus) soldanella

Classification: Angiospermae – Dicotyledones; Convolvulaceae

Habitat: Sandy and shingly shores, sand dune systems

Distribution: Atlantic and Mediterranean coasts of Europe and northern Africa; Indian Ocean coasts of Asia and Australasia; Atlantic and Pacific coasts of North and South America

Season: Flowers June to August

Description: Fleshy white rhizomes spread underground over considerable distances, while above ground prostrate slender stems may spread up to 1m (39 in) across the sand, rarely climbing other vegetation. Leaves fleshy, rich green, carried on stalks up to 10cm (4 in) long, kidney- or heart-shaped with a smooth margin.

Flowers borne on rectangular stems 10cm (4 in) or more long, petals fused into a bell-shaped funnel up to 5cm (2 in) in diameter, usually pink with white stripes. Five long white stamens. Base of calyx surrounded by large oblong bracteoles. Unopened buds are pointed and resemble a furled umbrella. Perennial.

General Remarks: Most of the Convolvulaceae are rambling or climbing plants with white latex-like sap. The majority of the 1,000 species are tropical, but some are temperate in the genera *Convolvulus* and *Calystegia* (bindweeds) and *Cuscuta* (dodders). The latter are parasitic annuals attached to and drawing nutrient from their host by means of suckers. Most of the *Convolvulus* species are rampant weeds of waste places, hedgerows and ill-kept gardens, often swamping other plants by their rapid growth.

The *Calystegia* species have similar habits to *Convolvulus*, and are structurally similar except for having broad stigmas and large bracteoles wrapped round the calyx.

SEA LAVENDER

Limonium vulgare

Classification: Angiospermae –
Dicotyledones; Plumbaginaceae
Habitat: Muddy saltmarshes on sheltered sea coasts and in estuaries
Distribution: Coasts of western and southern Europe, northern Africa and North America
Season: Flowers June to October
Description: A robust branching woody stock arises from a tap root penetrating deeply into the saltmarsh. The leaves are grey-green, thick and fleshy, 4–12cm (2–6 in) long and confined to a basal but not flattened rosette. Thick fleshy stalks lead to

prominent midrib veins in leaves, which vary from elongate-ovate to spear-shaped, narrowing to a pointed tip. Flowering stalks grey-green, rigid and erect, branched, up to 30cm (12 in) high carrying ten or more flower spikes.

Flower spikes short, slightly curved, densely packed with flower-bearing spikelets in two parallel rows. Flowers tubular, upright, set in small toothed bracts. Five short pointed pinkish sepals closely surround five purple petals, each flower is about 8mm (⅓ in) across and 16mm (⅔ in) deep. Anthers whitish yellow, as long as petals. Perennial.

General Remarks: The Plumbaginaceae is a comparatively small family of specialist salt-tolerant coastal plants, best-known of which are the thrifts *Armeria* and the sea lavenders *Limonium*, both of which may be the dominant plants in their habitats.

Partly as a result of its salt tolerance, Sea Lavender has a robust structure which allows it to dry well while retaining its colour. In consequence it is popular in dried flower arrangements. Elsewhere in the family are found two genera containing several popular garden plants; *Plumbago* and *Ceratostigma*.

41

SEA PEA

Lathyrus japonicus (*L. maritimus*)

Classification: Angiospermae – Dicotyledones; Leguminosae
Habitat: Coastal shingle beaches
Distribution: Circumpolar, on the coasts of the Atlantic, Pacific and Arctic Oceans, in Europe, Russia, Asia and North America, penetrating south into temperate regions.
Seasons: Flowers May to August
Description: A spreading, low-growing scrambling plant with dark green fleshy, salt-resistant leaves, rarely rising more than 30cm (12 in) except in sheltered locations, but often covering areas of shingle 2m (7 ft) or more across. Its habit is ideally suited to keep desiccation by the wind to a minimum.

Leaves pinnate about 5cm (2 in) long, with three or four pairs of oval leaflets, ending in a short tendril, sometimes branched. Flowers in a truncated spike, five to fifteen in number, each about 15mm (¾ in) across, rich bluish purple. Seed pods pea-like, up to 5cm (2 in) long, dark green and fleshy, containing from four to eight seeds. Perennial.

General Remarks: The Leguminosae is a huge family with over 7,000 species in 430 genera, many of which have root nodules containing nitrogen-fixing bacteria. Its flowers are characteristically butterfly-like, with a large erect standard petal, two lateral petals forming the wings, and a pair of lower petals, often joined by their lower margins, forming the keel.

The fruit is usually spherical and carried in an elongated pod as in the peas and beans. The family contains trees in genera such as *Robinia* and *Laburnum*, shrubs like gorse (*Ulex*), the clovers, medicagos, vetches and lupins. The Leguminosae contains perhaps the widest range of plants useful to man.

Potentilla anserina

Classification: Angiospermae – Dicotyledones; Rosaceae
Habitat: Road and track verges, field margins, dunes, damp pastures, open wasteland, cultivated arable fields.
Distribution: Temperate and cool temperate areas, occasionally subarctic zones, throughout Europe and Asia; Iceland, south to Spain, Italy and the Caucasus, through the Himalayas to Manchuria and Japan; North America south to New Jersey and northern California; Greenland, southern Australia and New Zealand
Season: Flowers from May to August or September, latest in colder latitudes

Description: A thick overwintering stock supports a compressed rosette of leaves, and in spring produces numerous creeping, rooting and ultimately flowering stolons over a radius of up to 1m (39 in). Leaves pinnate, green above with varying degrees of silvery hairiness, silver and hairy below. Overall length up to 25cm (10 in) with up to 12 pairs of major leaflets alternating with pairs of tiny ones. Main leaflets narrowly oval, with deeply serrated margins.

Flowers five-petalled, rich yellow, 25mm (1 in) in diameter, solitary, borne on long slender reddish stems arising from leaf axils. Insect pollinated. Perennial.

General Remarks: One of the most naturally cosmopolitan of all plants. While some potentillas are useful as ornamental garden plants and others are used in strawberry breeding programmes, the Silverweed, though attractive in many of its locations, can be properly classified as a weed in many agricultural circumstances.

Together with *Potentilla reptans*, the Creeping Cinquefoil of Europe, introduced accidentally but widely to North America, it is notoriously difficult to control.

SUNDEW

Drosera rotundifolia

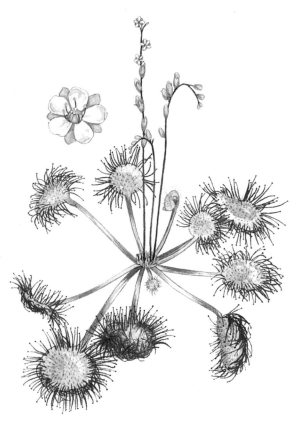

Classification: Angiospermae – Dicotyledones; Droseraceae

Habitat: Bogs, moorland and heathland pool margins and swampy areas, often characterized by the presence of sphagnum moss, normally on peaty or acidic soils

Distribution: Throughout Europe north of the Mediterranean basin, central and northern Asia, temperate and subarctic North America

Season: Flowers June to August

Description: A low-growing herb with all its leaves in a prostrate or slightly raised rosette. Leaves circular, about 10mm (²/₅ in) diameter, with petioles up to 3cm (1¼ in) long. Leaves pale green, but appearing red due to a profusion of glistening, club-shaped red glandular hairs.

Flowering spike erect, rarely more than 20cm (8 in) tall, usually carrying 12 or fewer five- or six-petalled white flowers about 6mm (¼ in) in diameter. Seeds small, winged to assist disposal. Perennial.

General Remarks: The small family Droseraceae contains about 100 species grouped in four genera. All are plants of acid, sandy, boggy or peaty soils, characteristically lacking in nutrients. These carnivorous plants remedy this deficiency by trapping insects on glandular leaf hairs and slowly digesting them, thus obtaining vital nutrients. The glandular hairs serve to attract the insects, trap them in the sticky secretions, and supply the enzyme-rich digestive juices.

The genus *Drosera* contains almost all of the species, and is remarkably cosmopolitan for plants with such an unusual and specialized lifestyle as it occurs in both the New World and the Old, being specially prolific in Africa and Australasia.

Classification: Angiospermae – Monocotyledones; Trilliaceae (Liliaceae)

Habitat: Moist broad-leaved woodlands with shaded conditions and deep leafmould-rich soil, calcareous rocks

Distribution: Native to eastern North America; introduced and occasionally naturalized in western Europe

Description: A family distinguished by having all parts in threes; leaves, sepals and petals. Flowering stems rise in clumps, flowering 25–30cm (10–12 in) tall, from creeping rhizomes, carrying three broadly oval, pointed leaves, greyish green with conspicuous parallel veins.

The flowers, about 5–7cm (2–3 in) in diameter, are borne singly on stems above the circlet of leaves. Each has three strikingly white, oval petals, often reflexed, also with parallel venation, supported by three broadly spear-shaped, green sepals. With time, the petals develop a pinkish flush. The six golden anthers and stamens are prominent in the throat of the flower. Fruit a conspicuous red, purple or black spherical berry up to 1cm (⅖ in) diameter, carried above the remains of the sepals. Perennial.

General Remarks: The name Trilliaceae indicates both a close link to the Liliaceae (in which family it is often included) and a distinction because of the *tri*-radial symmetry. Strangely, the European representative of the Trilliaceae, Herb Paris (*Paris quadrifolia*), has its leaves, sepals, petals and seeds arranged in fours, as its specific name implies.

Several members of this small, predominantly North American family have been taken successfully into cultivation, and make beautiful additions to any woodland garden, even if they may be slow to establish. Particular favourites are *T. erectum* and *T. sessile*.

WILD STRAWBERRY

Fragaria vesca

Classification: Angiospermae – Dicotyledones; Rosaceae

Habitat: Woodland, scrub and grassland, usually on calcareous soils; sometimes in montane regions

Distribution: Widely distributed through Europe and Asia east to Lake Baikal, on the Atlantic islands of Madeira and the Azores, and in eastern North America

Season: Flowers April to July

Description: A woody stock produces long runners rooting freely at the nodes and tips to develop new plantlets (the usual means of commercial strawberry bulk propagation). Leaves compound, with three leaflets of roughly equal size, bluntly oval, with deeply serrated margins, up to 6cm (2 in) in length, bright green above, grey-green below with fine silver hairs.

Flower stems erect, up to 30cm (12 in) high, usually branched and carrying several flowers on slender stems. Flowers five-petalled, white, up to 18mm (¾ in) in diameter. Fruit a fleshy receptacle – the strawberry – up to 2cm (¾ in) long, the surface covered in seeds, dispersed by fruit-eating birds. Perennial.

General Remarks: Though the fruit of the Wild Strawberry is delicious in itself (particularly the Alpine Strawberry), this and other *Fragaria* species are best known as parents in the breeding lines of modern strawberry cultivars. Fruit breeders have exploited characteristics in the fruit, and in the day-length sensitivity of the plants to create the modern strawberry-growing industry, where continuity of cropping is expected from March until October in the Northern Hemisphere.